# Quick Explanations of the Role of Court, Child Abuse, and the Role of Parents in Sharing Custody

L. C. Morgan

This book demonstrates an impressive personal improvement tool. It is not a substitute for working with qualified licensed clinical staff in psychotherapy. Nothing contained herein is meant to replace qualified legal, medical, or mental health advice. The author urges the reader to use these techniques under the supervision of a qualified therapist or physician. The author and publisher do not assume responsibility for how the reader chooses to apply the techniques herein. Readers are advised to consult with their physician, attorney, or other licensed professional practitioner before implementing any suggestions that follow. This book is not intended to take the place of sound professional advice, legal, medical, mental, or otherwise. Neither the author nor the publisher assumes any liability for possible adverse consequences because of the informational constrained within.

**Book Overview:**   Quick Explanations of the Role of Court, Child Abuse and the Role of Parents in Sharing Custody is part of the Quick Books Series to discuss information in shared custody and parenting. This information is shared to help families who are going through the process of sharing custody, going to family law court, and making sure your child or children has the best quality of life possible. Each parent has the responsibility to strengthen their family so that the generations that come after will have mental health, strong foundation in community, and build a better community with stronger foundations of healing.  By reading this book, the reader will:

- Learn about the types of court and its function.
- Learn how child abuse is defined.
- Learn about mental health and the impact of family conflict on children.
- Learn how to improve communication and utilizing court orders to document parental responsibilities and agreements.
- Improve mental health and well-being for your children.

**First published March 2023.**
**ISBN:  9798386284367**
**PAPERBACK EDITION**

## Dedication:

To the parents and stepparents that model a healthy way to share children and show love.

# Table of Contents

A LETTER TO PARENTS ABOUT COURTS, CHILD ABUSE, AND THE ROLE OF PARENTS...................................................................................9

ROLE OF COURT: FAMILY LAW, DEPENDENCY, CRIMINAL PROTECTION ORDERS, AND PROBATE GUARDIANSHIP ...........................13

WHAT IS CHILD ABUSE........................................................................28

ROLES OF PARENTS IN RAISING THE CHILDREN ..........................45

WHAT IS MENTAL HEALTH, WHO ARE THE PROVIDERS, AND WHY IS IT IMPORTANT?.......................................................................................60

TYPES OF TRAUMATIC EXPERIENCES.............................................65

COMMUNITY RESOURCES .................................................................69

EMERGENCY RESPONSE NUMBERS.................................................71

ADDITIONAL RESOURCES .................................................................75

SAMPLE FAMILY RULES.....................................................................76

ABOUT THE AUTHOR .........................................................................77

ABOUT DOTERRA ...............................................................................78

OTHER BOOKS BY THE AUTHOR......................................................79

# A LETTER TO PARENTS ABOUT COURTS, CHILD ABUSE, AND THE ROLE OF PARENTS

Dear Parents, Stepparents, and Guardians:

This is a difficult time for you and your family as you go through the process of custody negotiations, going to family law court, and making sure your child or children have the best quality of life possible. Maybe this comes as part of a breakup from a relationship or a one-night stand. Maybe this is after years of marriage. This "quick book" was released to inform parents, stepparents, and caregivers about the role of courts, child abuse, and the role of parents. The full book will be released later *(First version is called Tales From the Hood: Tips and Strategies for Sharing Custody With a Parent You Don't Like)*. However, for now, I wanted an immediate version on the role courts, what is child abuse, and the role of parents immediately available because of the confusion out in the world. This process of shared parenting is difficult, especially when you do not like them and are still very angry with the other parent. I am also here to remind you that your child's mental and emotional well-being should be your top priority as they are vital members of the community and will live your legacy in the future generations.

You can control only your response to the situation and how you model a healthy response for your child/children. It is important that you are the BIGGER person, modeling what is right. This means taking the time to talk with your child about their feelings, thoughts, emotions, and experiences. This also means to give them the space to express themselves without judgment so that you provide your child with a sense of security and stability by creating a regular routine and ensuring that their basic needs are met.

The original purpose of family is to provide a safe and supportive environment for its members to learn, grow, and thrive. Family members typically provide emotional, physical, and financial support to each other, as well as a sense of belonging and unity. Families offer guidance, stability and security amidst the ever-changing world. When families experience "division" of the values, customs, and vision that originally brought two people together, it causes a disruption in a secure foundation.

Shared parenting and co-parenting is an arrangement in which two parents work together to raise their children in a mutually supportive environment. This type of parenting arrangement focuses on both parents having an active role in their children's lives. It involves both parents having equal access to the children, and making decisions together about how to raise the children. This can involve shared parenting time, shared decision-making, and shared responsibilities. It is an important option for parents who are separated or divorced, but it can also be beneficial for parents who are still together. Shared parenting and co-parenting can help to create a more balanced, supportive family dynamic that is beneficial for all members of the family.

There are many reasons why parenting conflict does occur. Here are just a few:

- Different parenting styles – Parents may have different approaches to parenting, which can lead to disagreements and conflict.
- Financial issues – When money is tight, it can be difficult for parents to agree on how to allocate resources.

- Lack of communication – When parents do not talk to each other about their concerns, it can cause misunderstandings and build up tension.
- Different values and beliefs –Parents may not agree on certain values or beliefs, which can cause conflict.
- Stress and exhaustion –Parenting is a demanding job, and when parents are feeling overwhelmed, it can lead to conflict.
- Relationship Breakup-When parents break up and they have difficulty separating the relationship from the duties and obligations of parenting.

These are just some of the examples for parental conflict. However, the key reason for ongoing parenting conflict is unresolved Relationship Stressors. Romantic relationships can be stressful at times due to the intensity of emotions involved. Common stressors include communication issues, trust issues, lack of trust, jealousy, financial problems, and differences in values or beliefs. It is important to address these stressors early on in a relationship and to develop healthy communication and problem-solving strategies to keep the relationship strong. When the relationship cannot be salvaged, the two who may have children in common, become the focal point of stress.

Your child's mental and physical health is linked to how you and the other parent work together to minimize conflict in the home and to provide consistency for your child. This will help them feel less overwhelmed and better understand the situation. Along with the partnerships with the stepparents, grandparents, and extended family are responsible for helping the child form a healthy identity, and create a circle of support.

Finally, I encourage you to reach out for professional help if needed. Talking to a counselor or therapist can be extremely beneficial for your child's mental and emotional health.

I hope this "quick book" will be a useful resource for you and your family. I wish you the best during this difficult time.

Sincerely,

LaLisa Morgan, LCSW
Lead Clinician and Program Administrator
Kingdom Journey to Healing a program of
Generations 1865: Counseling, Consulting, and Coaching

# ROLE OF COURT: FAMILY LAW, DEPENDENCY, CRIMINAL PROTECTION ORDERS, AND PROBATE GUARDIANSHIP

The role of the court in family law, dependency, criminal protection orders, child support court, and probate guardianship is to ensure that the rights of all parties are protected and respected in a fair and just manner. Family law covers a wide range of legal matters, such as divorce, child custody and support, adoption, and pre- and post-nuptial (marriage) agreements. Dependency covers matters related to the care and protection of children, such as guardianships and juvenile court proceedings. Criminal protection orders are court orders that protect victims of domestic violence or other criminal activity from the perpetrator. Child Support Court covers the financial support for the child or children. Lastly, Probate Guardianship involves the court appointing a guardian for an incapacitated person or minor. In all of these areas, the court's main responsibility is to ensure the safety and rights of all parties are respected, while also making decisions in a timely and ethical manner.

Family Law is the area of law that deals with legal issues related to family relationships, such as marriage, divorce, adoption, child support, and child custody. It also covers issues related to inheritance, spousal support, and estate planning. Family Law Court provides invaluable legal advice and assistance to individuals, couples, and families. Family law will also address domestic violence cases when children are involved to ensure the rights of parents. In family law court, a judge will make rulings based on the best interest of the child, and strive to ensure that all parties involved have their rights protected and respected.

The role of the court in a child custody case is to make a decision that is in the best interest of the child. A court will consider factors such as the child's age, mental and physical health, emotional and educational needs of the child, child's relationship with each parent, the parents' lifestyle, the parents' ability to provide a stable home environment, and the child's preferences. The court may also consider any history of domestic violence or child abuse. Ultimately, the court will make a decision that is in the child's best interest. Sometimes, the court will also ask a social worker to help with clarifying what are the best interest of the child and then the court will make a final court order (ruling) that is recommended. This court order can be modified at the child's different ages and stages. So the court order evolves with the child if you are proactively engaging the court to find solutions.

A Family Time Plan, also known as Visitation Plan, is an agreement between two or more family members or guardians that outlines the times and dates that each member can spend with their children or other family members during a certain period of time.

Family Time Plan is not a child support order, and whether or not the person pays child support, they legally the right to visit and spend time with their child. Visitation court orders are legal orders issued by a court that grant one parent or guardian the right to visit or spend time with the children or other family members during a certain period of time. These court orders are typically used in cases where the parents or guardians have a custody dispute or when a parent or guardian is not able to care for the children and visitation rights are granted to a third party (for example, grandparents). Both family time plans and visitation court orders are important to ensure that children are able to spend quality time with all of their family members in a safe, secure, and supportive environment. Family law is incredibly broad and can encompass a variety of matters, including marriage and divorce, adoptions, paternity and child support, child custody and visitation, alimony and spousal support, and more.

Probate guardianship is a type of guardianship in which a person (the guardian) is appointed by a court to make decisions regarding the care, custody, and finances of a minor or incapacitated adult. The guardian is responsible for the well-being of the ward (child) and must act in the ward's best interest. The court will generally appoint a probate guardian after considering the child's wishes, the ability of the guardian to provide proper care, and the potential benefits of guardianship. Parents can appoint a relative or friend to take temporary guardianship of a child or children. If a parent passes away, he or she can appoint a guardian as long as the other parent is not able or willing to take on the parental role.

A Criminal Protective Order (also known as a restraining order) is a court order issued by a judge to protect a person from being abused, harassed, stalked, or threatened by another person. The order requires the individual to stay a certain distance away from the protected person, as well as refrain from contacting them in any way.

A Criminal Protective Order is designed to keep the protected individual safe and can be issued to protect an individual from a family member, a romantic partner, or anyone else with whom the protected person has had a relationship with. At times, children are also listed as protected parties. This will be clearly documented on the court order. Otherwise, the protected parent will need to file Family Law paperwork to address primary custodial parent, non-custodial parent, and visitation rights. The restraining order does not end parental rights. Additional court documentation is needed so both fathers and mothers are equally protected.

Child Support Court is another court when family law has not made an order for financial support. This determines the financial responsibilities of the custodial and the non-custodial parent. Yes, this is another courtroom. However, often times, Family Law will make the initial court order, and you can ask the

State local agency to enforce the court order, via garnishment of wages. This does NOT change the custodial arrangement and is NOT a reason to discontinue family visitation with your child. By law, both parents must support their children and parents must share the financial responsibility for raising their children. Sometimes parents can agree on how to share this responsibility without going to court. If you and the other parent can't agree, you can ask the court for a child support order.

Child Support Court also monitors financial support throughout the life of the child or children. Child support is determined by the court based on the income of each parent and the amount of money that a court tells a parent to pay every month. This money is to help pay for the children's living expenses. It is not a punishment to the other parent. It is designed to give the basic necessities for the child or children to have a minimal standard quality of life. Usually, child support is paid to the person primarily caring for the children, or primary custodial parent. But, there may be exceptions based on how much each parent earns. Additional considerations in the order depends on how many children that the money must be split between to maximize support to each child. The money is for the child and not a spousal support to the other parent. Both men and woman can be the custodial parent and receive the funds.

A child support order will say how the parents share the financial responsibility. It can also require an employer to deduct the support directly from a paycheck. The duty to pay support typically ends when a child turns 18 and graduates high school. Most children have to graduate by the age of 22 if they have special education services. If they're still in high school full-time and cannot support themselves, the duty ends when they graduate or turn 22, whichever happens first. The duty to pay child support ends when a child gets married, enters a domestic partnership, joins the military, is emancipated, or dies. The duty to pay child support can be extended longer, if the child is disabled and cannot support itself or if the parents agree for support to continue. Sometimes the child can access disability income in lieu of child support. When the custodial parent receives state assistance, the child support will often go to the state agency and NOT the custodial parent. You must refer to your local state or county for additional details.

Superior Courts are helpful for child custody matters for safety and well-being of the child. Court is a necessary step to ensure the safety and well-being of a child in child custody matters. It is important to remember that the court is there to ensure the best outcome for the child and to act in their best interest. It is also important to be aware that court proceedings can be lengthy and complex, so it is important to seek legal advice from a qualified lawyer to ensure that the desired outcome is achieved. Here are a few benefits of utilizing the courts:

- Family law courts provide a neutral forum where both parents can present their case for custody.
- Issue orders to protect the safety and welfare of children involved in a custody case.
- Address the best interests of the child when deciding on a custody arrangement.
- Order supervised visitation or relocation when necessary.
- Grant temporary custody to one parent while the case is pending.
- Order the exchange of relevant financial documents.
- Set a parenting plan that outlines the responsibilities of each parent.
- Order a psychological or psychiatric evaluation for the parents or children.
- Order mediation or counseling sessions for the parents.
- Order a child custody evaluation if necessary.
- Appoint a guardian ad litem (minor's attorney) to represent the interests of the children.
- Order payment of child support and spousal support.
- Order the transfer of parental rights or the termination of parental rights.
- Order a parenting time schedule that includes holidays and school breaks.
- Order the exchange of relevant medical and educational documents.

- Order a parent to undergo substance abuse testing or evaluation.
- Order the creation of a parenting plan to be followed by both parents.
- Order the exchange of tax documents and other financial records.
- Order a paternity test if necessary.
- Order counseling or therapy for the children.

Court orders can be helpful in reducing parental conflict by ensuring that both parents are clear on their parental rights and responsibilities regarding the care and upbringing of their children. Court orders can also provide a framework for parents to communicate and cooperate in making decisions about their children. Additionally, court orders can help to clarify the roles of each parent and provide a sense of security for the children, by ensuring that both parents are held accountable for their actions. It is important to note, however, that court orders are not a substitute for communication and cooperation between the parents, and it is still important to attempt to resolve issues between parents without having to resort to court orders. Conjoint counseling can help both parties learn to communicate effectively in regards to the child's needs. You can request a free consultation for Conjoint Counseling by going to www.kingdomjourney2healing.com.

Parental conflict is when parents are unable to agree on decisions or how to handle a situation. It can range from minor disagreements to serious disputes that affect the entire family.

Parental conflict can have a negative impact on children, leading to feelings of insecurity, guilt, and stress. It is important for parents to learn how to effectively communicate with each other and work together to resolve conflicts in a healthy manner. Parent conflict can occur for a variety of reasons, such as differing values, financial problems, or a lack of communication and understanding. It may be caused by stressors outside the family, such as work-related issues, and can lead to tension and arguments between parents. Conflict can also be caused by changes in the family dynamic, such as a new baby or a child leaving home. Parental conflict can occur when parents are not having open and honest conversations to discuss their issues and work towards a resolution. Here are barriers in communication that cause parental conflict:

- Lack of communication: Not communicating with parents, stepparents, or guardians can lead to a breakdown in the relationship.
- Different beliefs: When parents, stepparents, or guardians have different beliefs, it can create tension.
- Unreasonable expectations: Having unrealistic expectations from parents, stepparents, or guardians can lead to disappointment.

- Power struggles: When parents, stepparents, or guardians try to exert too much power over their children, it can lead to conflict.
- Differing parenting styles: When parents, stepparents, or guardians have different parenting styles, it can be difficult for the child to adjust.
- Disagreements over decision-making: When parents, stepparents, or guardians disagree on how decisions should be made, it can lead to discord.
- Lack of trust: When parents, stepparents, or guardians don't trust their children, it can create tension.
- Unresolved issues: Holding on to unresolved issues from the past can make it difficult to have a healthy relationship with parents, stepparents, or guardians.
- Unhealthy boundaries: When parents, stepparents, or guardians have unhealthy boundaries, it can lead to conflict.
- Conflict avoidance: Avoiding conflict can lead to underlying issues never being addressed and can create tension in the relationship.

Reducing parental conflict is essential for creating a healthy and positive environment for children to grow up in and it is a great goal for parents, stepparents, and guardians. Parental conflict can have a negative impact on a child's mental and emotional well-being, as well as their physical health. It can lead to feelings of insecurity, sadness and even anger in children.

The key is to ensure that each individual is given the opportunity to communicate their feelings, concerns, and perspectives in a constructive manner. By reducing parental conflict, parents can ensure that their children have the best possible start in life and can grow up to be emotionally and mentally healthy adults. Here are some tips to help reduce conflict:

- Make sure to set aside designated time for each person to express their thoughts and feelings.
- Encourage open dialogue between all members of the family, and do your best to listen without judgment.
- Try not to jump to conclusions or make assumptions about someone else's feelings or intentions.
- Be willing to compromise and work together to find solutions that are beneficial for everyone.
- Respect each other's boundaries and be understanding when someone needs time and space.
- If a disagreement arises, focus on the issue at hand, rather than attacking the character of the other person.
- Develop and maintain a sense of trust between all members of the family.
- Set a good example by treating everyone with kindness, respect, and understanding.

Parental conflict can have a significant and lasting impact on a child's mental wellness. It can cause feelings of insecurity, fear, and guilt, and can lead to long-term mental health issues such as depression, anxiety, or post-traumatic stress disorder.

Research has shown that children who are exposed to parental conflict are more likely to experience poor academic performance, have difficulty forming and maintaining relationships, and display aggressive or disruptive behavior. Parents can reduce the impact of their conflict on their child's mental wellness by managing their disagreements in a respectful and non-confrontational manner, avoiding the use of punitive or aggressive tactics, and ensuring that the child's needs are taken into consideration. Additionally, parental conflict impact children in other ways:

- Children may be exposed to feelings of insecurity and fear as they witness their parents arguing.
- Children may experience feelings of guilt, believing that they are the cause of the conflict.
- Children may develop anxiety or depression as a result of their parents' conflict.
- Children may be less likely to succeed in school when their parents are in conflict.
- Children may struggle to form relationships with peers and adults if they are exposed to their parents arguing.
- Children may experience physical health problems due to their parents' conflict.
- Children may be more prone to aggressive behavior and have difficulty managing their emotions.
- Children may develop low self-esteem when exposed to their parents arguing.
- Children may struggle to trust others, leading to difficulty forming and maintaining relationships.
- Children may become more withdrawn and isolated when exposed to their parents' conflict.
- Parents often have different expectations for their children, which can lead to disagreements and conflict.
- Child may suffer when money is often a source of conflict, especially when it comes to parenting.
- Parents who have different parenting approaches may find it hard to agree and compromise and cause confusion for the children.

- Children learn poor communication as a result of parents who don't communicate effectively, issues can easily become misunderstood, leading to conflict.
- Children learn a lack of Respect: Respect is key in any relationship and it can easily be lost in parenting.
- Children get confused and further a lack understanding of adult issues: If one parent doesn't understand why the other is doing something, it can lead to conflict.
- Children have divided loyalty when the other parent is involved too much in child's relationship dynamic with the other parent, creating tension and stress, especially if the other parent feels like their input is not being valued.
- Child can develop lack of Self-Awareness as the parents, who are unaware of their own emotions and reactions, struggle to remain calm and rational during conflicts.
- Children develop a lack of trust and support due to ongoing parental conflict.

Using the court can be incredibly helpful for parents, stepparents and guardians as it provides a formal process to reach a legally binding agreement. The court is able to consider the best interests of any children involved, and make orders that are tailored to the individual circumstances. Additionally, the court provides an impartial and neutral setting, allowing parents to focus on the issues at hand, rather than worrying about how their emotions may be affecting the process. Ultimately, the court can help parents to reach an agreement that is beneficial for everyone. Mothers and Fathers are notorious for saying we need the government out of our business. In this case, families need courts to find healthy solutions for parental disagreements so the child or children enjoy the benefits of both parents.

# WHAT IS CHILD ABUSE

Child Abuse is a very sensitive topic in many American communities. Unfortunately, child welfare agencies across the nation have continued traumatizing families with disproportional treatment as to allegations of child abuse and how investigations are handled. So it important that families do not call child welfare agencies on each other fraudulently and cause trauma to your family. So let me take the time here to explain what child abuse truly is.

The effects of child abuse can be long-term effect and this is considered Adverse Childhood Experiences (ACES). As a reminder, ACES is defined as any traumatic event that occurs during childhood that has a lasting, negative effect on the individual's physical, psychological, or social well-being. ACEs can include physical, sexual, or emotional abuse, neglect, family disruption, substance misuse, or violence. ACEs can have long-term penalties or consequences, leading to chronic health conditions, mental health issues, and other problems. Children who are physically abused and neglected may suffer immediate physical injuries such as cuts, bruises, or broken bones. They may also have emotional and psychological problems, such as depression, anxiety or posttraumatic stress. Parental conflict, lack of the ability for two parents to share custody peaceful, can cause long stress that impacts the mental health of the children. Additionally, children who are abused or neglected are also at increased risk for experiencing future violence victimization and perpetration, substance abuse, sexually transmitted infections, delayed brain development, lower educational attainment, and limited employment opportunities. Chronic abuse may result in toxic stress, which can change brain development and increase the risk for problems like posttraumatic stress disorder and learning, attention, and memory difficulties.

The federal definition of child abuse and neglect is outlined in the Child Abuse Prevention and Treatment Act (CAPTA). According to CAPTA, child abuse and neglect is defined as "any recent act or failure to act on the part of a parent or caretaker which results in death, serious physical or emotional harm, sexual abuse or exploitation; or an act or failure to act which presents an imminent risk of serious harm." This definition includes acts of physical violence, neglect, emotional abuse, and sexual abuse. The federal definition is the minimum standard while each state will have additional laws and rules to support local enforcement of child safety. Federal legislation provides guidance to States by identifying a minimum set of acts or behaviors that define child abuse and neglect. The Federal Child Abuse Prevention and Treatment Act (CAPTA) (42 U.S.C.A. § 5106g), as amended by the CAPTA Reauthorization Act of 2010, defines child abuse and neglect as, at minimum:

- "Any recent act or failure to act on the part of a parent or caretaker, which results in death, serious physical or emotional harm, sexual abuse or exploitation"; or

- "An act or failure to act which presents an imminent risk of serious harm."

- This definition of child abuse and neglect refers specifically to parents and other caregivers. A "child" under this definition generally means a person who is younger than age 18 or who is not an emancipated minor.

Federal legislation sets minimum standards for States that accept Federal funding, each State is responsible for defining child maltreatment in State law. Definitions of child abuse and neglect are typically located in two places within each State's statutory code:

- Civil statutes provide definitions of child maltreatment to guide individuals who are mandated to identify and report suspected child abuse and determine the grounds for intervention by State child protection agencies and civil courts. Locate definitions for your State by conducting a State Statues Search on the Information Gateway website.

- Criminal statutes define those forms of child maltreatment that can subject an offender to arrest and prosecution in criminal courts.

There are four major types of maltreatment in their definitions: neglect, physical abuse, sexual abuse, and emotional abuse or neglect. However, there are also many subcategories. A mandated reporter is a person who is required to report known or suspected instances of child abuse and/or neglect if they, in their professional capacity or within the scope of their employment, observe a child who appears to be a victim of abuse, neglect, or exploitation. Failure to report can lead to severe penalties including jail time and fines. There are many people required by law to report suspicion of abuse and they do so because of the law or face harsh penalties based on a suspicion. Unfortunately, families where a child is disabled and communities of color experience an excessive amount of reporting compared to children who are White or Asian descent.

Child abuse cases, when legitimate, is heartbreaking and it is important to remember that no child deserves to experience any type of abuse, physical, emotional, or otherwise. If you or someone you know is a victim of child abuse, please reach out for help. There are many resources available, including hotlines, counseling, and legal services. Together, we can work to end this horrible form of abuse and create a safe environment for children everywhere. Child abuse reporting is essential in protecting children and teens from harm and it is pivotal of a thriving community. It allows victims of abuse to receive help and support, as well as allowing authorities to investigate and take legal action against perpetrators and promote healing within a family system. Reporting abuse also serves as public safety with the goal to increase public awareness and highlight the issue of child abuse, allowing society to take steps to prevent it from occurring in the future. By reporting abuse, we are helping to create a safer, more supportive environment for all children. To summarize what is Child Abuse, or Child Maltreatment falls into two categories:

- Any act or series of acts of commission or
- Act of omission by a parent or other caregiver

The results of child abuse must be significant as to the harm, potential for harm, or threat of harm to a child or children.

## *Acts of Commission (Child Abuse)*

This can be defined as words or overt actions that cause harm, potential harm, or threat of harm to a child. Acts of commission are deliberate and intentional. This behavior often causes harm to a child which may or may not be the intended as a consequence. Intentionality only applies to the caregivers' acts—not the consequences of those acts. For example, a caregiver may intend to hit a child as punishment for discipline purposes (i.e., hitting the child is not accidental or unintentional) but not intend to cause the child to have a concussion. The following types of maltreatment involve acts of commission:

- Physical abuse
- Sexual abuse
- Psychological abuse

## Acts of Omission (Child Neglect)

The failure to provide for a child's basic physical, emotional, or educational needs or to protect a child from harm or potential harm. Like acts of commission, harm to a child may or may not be the intended consequence. The following types of maltreatment involve acts of omission:

- Failure to provide
- Physical neglect
- Emotional neglect
- Medical/dental neglect
- Educational neglect
- Failure to supervise
- Inadequate supervision
- Exposure to violent environments

For additional clarity, Intimate Partner or Domestic Violence also falls in the category of child abuse by way of General Neglect and Emotional Abuse. Intimate partner and domestic violence can have a serious detrimental impact on the safety and well-being of a child. Not only can physical and sexual abuse be inflicted, but children can also be exposed to general neglect and emotional abuse, such as witnessing violence between their parents or caregivers. This type of exposure can lead to serious psychological and behavioral problems, including depression, anxiety, social withdrawal, aggression, and decreased academic performance. It is important to recognize the signs of domestic violence and to seek help if you, or someone you know, is in an abusive relationship. There are many resources available to help those affected by intimate partner and domestic violence, so don't hesitate to reach out.

Domestic violence and intimate partner violence are both forms of abuse that take place between two people in an intimate relationship. Domestic violence can include physical, sexual, emotional, financial, and psychological abuse, while intimate partner violence typically refers to physical and sexual violence. Domestic violence can affect people of all genders, ages, races, ethnicities, and socioeconomic backgrounds.

The goal of domestic violence is to gain power and control over the other person. Intimate partner violence can have a devastating effect on the victim's physical and mental health, as well as their ability to trust and form relationships. It is important to understand the signs of domestic violence and to seek help if you or someone you know is a victim. And yes, men and women have been victims of intimate partner violence. The female as well as men can initiate intimate partner abuse. It is important to understand that both parties deserve safety. Either partner in a relationship, regardless of gender, can perpetrate intimate partner abuse. It is important to remember that regardless of the gender of the abuser, victims may experience physical, emotional, psychological, and financial abuse. It is important to provide help and support to survivors of abuse, and to create and maintain safe and respectful relationships. The cycle of violence in domestic violence consists of six distinct behaviors:

- Tension Building – during this phase, a perpetrator may start to feel tense and display signs of irritation or aggression.
- Incident – during this phase, the perpetrator may act out their feelings of tension and aggression through physical, emotional, psychological, or sexual abuse of the victim.
- Reconciliation/Honeymoon – during this phase, the perpetrator may apologize or make promises of change in order to retain control of the victim.
- Calm – during this phase, the victim and perpetrator may have a period of relative peace and calm.
- Escalation – during this phase, the tension and aggressive behavior of the perpetrator escalates to a higher level.
- Crisis – during this phase, the perpetrator's behavior may become more dangerous, and the victim may feel a sense of imminent danger.

Domestic violence can have a far-reaching and devastating impact on the adult relationships. It can cause physical and emotional pain, financial difficulties, and a sense of insecurity and fear. It can also lead to isolation, depression, and changes in behavior. Domestic violence can happen to anyone, regardless of race, gender, or age. It is essential to seek help and support if you or someone you know is in an abusive situation. There are resources available to assist individuals, couples, and families in getting out of an abusive relationship and finding safety and support. Negative behaviors that demonstrate abuse in relationships include coercive control, harassment, and physical violence are part of the cycle of domestic violence.

Coercive control is a pattern of behavior used by one person in a relationship to assert power and control over the other partner. It is a form of psychological abuse that includes behaviors such as intimidation, isolation, manipulation, humiliation, threats, and economic control. Coercive control can result in physical or sexual violence, but the primary goal is to control and manipulate the other person through fear and intimidation. Coercive control can have a devastating impact on the victim's mental health and well-being. Have you ever had a woman that controlled what time you leave or come home from work? Have you ever had a man who controlled how you spent your money? Do you have a partner that forces you to have sexual relations? These actions can be linked to coercive control.

Harassment is any kind of behavior that is unwanted, offensive, or threatening. It can be verbal, nonverbal, physical, or even written. It is typically considered a form of discrimination and can involve making offensive remarks or unwanted physical contact, as well as making threats or intimidating behavior. Harassment is illegal in many countries and can result in legal action. Harassment in the workplace include derogatory jokes, racial slurs, personal insults, and expressions of disgust or intolerance toward a particular race. However, harassment in the relationship could also include these types of verbal assaults, including someone telling you that you are "fat", "ugly", "busted and disgusted," and "no one wants you". It could even involve talking negatively about how you process your thoughts, emotions, and feelings.

Physical violence is any type of physical force or aggression used to harm another person. It can include hitting, pushing, kicking, slapping, and using objects as weapons. It can also involve psychological harm, such as threats and intimidation, as well as emotional abuse. Physical violence should never be tolerated in any form and should be addressed immediately. It is never okay to get into a physical altercation with another person. A man should not be hit or slapped by any woman. Most men won't even admit it under the guidelines of "masculinity." Nor, should any man strangle a woman.

Your safety and the safety of your children matters. If you are feeling threatened or in danger, the best thing to do is to remove yourself from the situation as quickly and safely as possible. If the situation is not safe for you to escape, it is important to remember that physical violence is never the answer. There are a variety of resources available to help you through such a difficult situation, such as a mental health professional, a hot line, or a helpline. You can request a free consultation for emotional support by going to www.kingdomjourney2healing.com.

Healing from the cycle of violence can provide a number of physical, mental, and emotional benefits. Physically, it can reduce stress, improve physical health, and help you to make healthier lifestyle choices. Mentally, it can help you to develop healthier coping skills, build resilience, and increase your sense of control over your life. Emotionally, it can help you to build meaningful relationships, develop self-esteem, and increase your overall sense of happiness and well-being. It can also help you to understand the reasons why violence is used and how to break the cycle of violence in the future.

Anger management is an important skill to have, especially when it comes to reducing the cycle of violence so that you can improve communication with the other parent. Learning how to better manage your emotions can help you to react more calmly in stressful situations and prevent you from escalating any conflict. It's important to practice mindful breathing, positive self-talk, and other calming strategies to help manage your anger in a way that promotes peace and understanding. Managing anger is key to having the opportunity to have clear communication. Here are a few anger management strategies:

- Take deep breaths and count to ten: Taking a few deep breaths and counting to ten can help you relax and take a step back from the situation.
- Take a break: If you feel that you are getting too angry, take a break and go to a different room or go for a walk.

- Think before you speak: Before you react to a situation, take a few seconds to think about how you want to respond.

- Practice relaxation techniques: Meditation, yoga, and other relaxation techniques can help you manage your anger by calming your body and mind.
- Talk it out: Talk to someone you trust about why you are angry and how you are feeling.
- Write it out: Writing down your thoughts and feelings can help you express your anger in a healthy way.
- Identify triggers: Identifying the things that trigger your anger can help you better manage it.
- Focus on the present: Don't let yourself get overwhelmed by thinking about past events or worrying about the future.
- Exercise: Exercise can help release tension and reduce stress, which can help you manage your anger.
- Seek professional help: If your anger is too intense or unmanageable, seek help from a therapist or counselor. You can request a free consultation for emotional support by going to www.kingdomjourney2healing.com.

Mastering your individuality is key. Your identity ensures your overall wellness and defines your self-esteem. You must first love yourself so that you can love others---and yes, you can't love your children well if you don't love you! Developing a strong sense of self-identity is essential for overall mental and emotional well-being. It can be helpful to consider the core values and beliefs that are important to you, as well as what makes you unique. Spending time alone allows you to get to know your own thoughts and be in touch with your spiritual identity. Taking time to focus on the things that you have accomplished and the skills that you possess can also be a great way to build self-confidence. Finally, surrounding yourself with supportive people who encourage you to be your true self and appreciate your individual qualities can help to create a strong sense of self-identity. Mastering your identity is an important part of self-discovery and growth. It can help you understand who you are, what your values and beliefs are, and how you want to live your life. By understanding your identity, you become empowered to make choices that are in alignment with your true self, which can lead to personal evolution, and truly master your individuality before exploring any future relationship.

Your evolution and healing is a process of change that is driven by natural selection. It is an ongoing process that affects the genetic makeup of species of humanity through the selection of favorable traits and the elimination of unfavorable traits.

Healing, on the other hand, is a process of repairing damage to the body caused by disease, injury, or trauma. It is a process of restoring the body to its normal functioning state and can involve a range of treatments from medication to talk therapy to surgery. Both evolution and healing can cause changes to an organism and are essential processes for the survival of species.

You define what your evolutionary healing looks like. Who are you? What kind of parent do you want to be as a person who truly loves him or herself? Take your time and just learn who you are so you don't impulsively make poor choices with poor emotional hygiene. Let's clean you up with defining your morals, values, and character. You can request a free consultation for emotional support by going to www.kingdomjourney2healing.com.

Communicating your underlying needs and desires is difficult, especially when you are uncertain about what they mean to you. The best way to start is to take some time to reflect on yourself and your relationships. Ask yourself what you need and desire, and then think about how you can communicate that in a respectful and constructive way. It may also help to talk to a trusted friend or counselor to help you identify and understand your underlying needs and desires. This is not taught in families. You must strategically unlearn unhealthy habits from your family of origin. As an adult, you get to apply wisdom and become the man or woman you want to be. Healing from the cycle of violence can help children in many ways with you becoming a healthy adult. It can provide your child with emotional relief, help them process and work through traumatic experiences, teach them coping skills, and give them a sense of safety. It can also help children build resilience and develop healthier relationships with themselves and others. Healing can provide children with an opportunity to explore their feelings, process difficult emotions, and learn how to better manage their reactions and responses in the future. Healing can also help children build trust in themselves and others, as well as foster their self-love and self-esteem. Ultimately, healing can help children to become more confident, secure, and successful in their lives. It is important to strengthen the community and it starts with loving yourself enough to ensure your own safety, mental and physical wellness, and fostering healthy adult relationships. Self-love is the foundation of building a strong and thriving families and the community. When we take the time to practice self-care and look out for our own safety and wellness, we create a space for healthy relationships with others. It's important to remember that in order for us to be strong together, we must first be strong within ourselves.

# ROLES OF PARENTS IN RAISING THE CHILDREN

Parents play a very important role in raising their children. They are responsible for providing love, guidance, support, and structure. They are responsible for helping their children develop into responsible, independent, and compassionate adults. Parents should be encouraging and supportive, provide appropriate discipline, and set clear boundaries. They should also help their children develop strong self-esteem, teach them good values, and help them learn problem-solving skills. Parents should also provide their children with a safe and secure environment, provide them with healthy meals, and ensure they get enough sleep. Ultimately, parents should strive to create a loving and nurturing home environment that allows children to thrive.

Having children is an incredible experience that can bring a lot of joy and fulfillment to our lives. Children can bring out the best in us, inspiring us to be more patient, understanding and compassionate. They can teach us valuable lessons about life and can even help us to become better versions of ourselves. Additionally, having children can help us to create a lasting legacy, as we pass down our values, beliefs, and knowledge to the next generation. Here are some more wonderful reasons that people have children:

- Brings immense joy and happiness to your life.
- Teaches you responsibility and helps you grow as a person.
- Gives you the opportunity to pass on your values and beliefs to the next generation.
- Bring families closer together.
- Brings fulfillment and purpose to your life.
- Gives you someone to love unconditionally.
- Helps you form strong relationships with other parents.
- Allows you to teach and nurture them as they grow.
- Gives you an opportunity to provide another life with opportunities and experiences.
- Gives you a chance to look at the world through their eyes and enjoy it in a whole new way.

Two-parent households on the same accord can provide many benefits for children. Having two parents in the home can provide a better balance of love, support, discipline and guidance, which can result in children having higher self-esteem, better academic performance, and a more secure feeling of being loved and accepted. Having two parents in the home also allows for parents to have a greater sense of stability in their relationship with each other. This can provide a more stable home environment for children, which can promote healthy development. Additionally, two-parent households can provide children with more financial security and more diverse life experiences, both of which can help them succeed in life. Here are some benefits of a two-parent household:

- Two parents can provide a more balanced approach to parenting, with each parent contributing unique perspectives, strengths, and skills.

- Two parents can provide more stability for children, as both parents can be available to support and guide children.

- Two parents can help provide better financial security, as two incomes can help cover expenses and provide more resources for the family.

- Two parents can provide more opportunities for children, such as access to extracurricular activities, travel, and other enrichment activities.

- Two parents can serve as role models for children, helping to instill values, morals, and life skills.

- Two parents can provide emotional support for each other and for their children, allowing for a healthier family environment.

- Two parents can help create a more nurturing home environment, with both parents expressing love, respect, and understanding for each other and for their children.

- Two parents can help teach children important life skills, such a problem solving, decision-making, and communication.

- Two parents can help promote a safe and secure home environment, where children feel loved and supported.

- Two parents can help foster a sense of belonging and connectedness within the family, allowing for a stronger bond among family members.

Single parenting, although sometimes difficult, is also a rewarding journey. To help you make it a successful experience, here are some tips. First, create a routine and stick to it. Having a consistent schedule can help keep your children and yourself on track. Secondly, make time for yourself. Taking care of yourself is important to be an effective parent, so find some time to relax and recharge. Thirdly, reach out for help. Do not be afraid to ask for help when you need it, whether it's from a family member, friend, or support group. Finally, give yourself grace. Parenting is difficult for everyone, so do not be too hard on yourself, and accept that you will make mistakes.

The role of the father is an important and integral part of any family. Fathers provide guidance, support, and love to their children. They may also take on the role of disciplinarian, providing instruction on acceptable behavior and setting boundaries. Fathers are often seen as the head of the household, taking on responsibilities such as making financial decisions, providing protection and safety, and fostering an environment of respect and caring. Fathers can also be a great source of comfort, offering a shoulder to cry on, a listening ear, and a safe place to turn to when times are tough. While each father's role is unique, the overall impact of a father's presence in a home is undeniable. The historical role of the father has been linked to the following:

1. Provide financial security: Fathers are often seen as the breadwinners of the family, and providing financial stability is a crucial role for many fathers.

2. Offer emotional support: Fathers can offer emotional support to their children by providing a safe and secure environment for them to grow and thrive.

3. Teach life skills: Fathers are often the ones teaching their children how to navigate the world and providing guidance on important life skills.

4. Create a strong bond: Fathers play a large role in forming strong bonds with their children and this helps foster a healthy relationship between the two.

5. Offer discipline: Fathers may be the ones offering discipline to their children, helping them to become responsible and respectful adults.

6. Provide structure: Fathers can help provide structure and routine to a household, which is important for children to learn structure and discipline.

7. Show respect: Fathers should show respect to their children, which

helps to build trust and foster good communication.

8. Be a role model: Fathers can be role models for their children, showing them how to behave in a positive and respectful way.

9. Support extracurricular activities: Fathers should support their children's extracurricular activities and interests to help them learn and grow.

10. Show unconditional love: Fathers should show unconditional love and acceptance to their children, no matter their mistakes or successes.

The historical role of the mother is essential to the growth and development of a child. As a mother, you are your child's first teacher, mentor, and source of love and security. You provide guidance and support, help them to develop their skills and abilities, and nurture them to become a confident and independent individual. You are also responsible for instilling values and teaching the importance of good character. Your role as a mother is to be a loving, caring, and supportive role model who helps shape your child into the best version of themselves.

Mothers play an incredibly important role in parenting. They are often the ones who provide the primary care, nurturing, and emotional support to their children. They are also typically responsible for ensuring that their children's basic needs are met, such as providing them with food, clothing, and a safe and comfortable home. Beyond the basics, mothers are also often the ones who teach their children values, morals, and how to navigate their world. They are often the primary source of discipline and the one who sets and enforces limits, while also providing their child with love and guidance. Mothers truly are the foundation of a family and the ones who make sure that their children grow up with the skills, knowledge, and values to become successful and well-adjusted adults. Here are a few ways that mothers are important:

1. Provide emotional support - Mothers are often the primary caregivers for their children and act as a source of comfort, reassurance, and emotional stability.

2. Instill values - Mothers have a unique role in teaching their children values, such as respect, honesty, and compassion.

3. Discipline - Mothers help their children learn behavioral boundaries and the importance of following rules and instructions.

4. Serve as a role model - Mothers provide an example of how to behave and act in different situations, and they can be a positive influence in their children's lives.

5. Give unconditional love - Mothers love their children unconditionally and provide them with a sense of security and acceptance.

6. Provide a safe environment - Mothers work to create a safe, secure, and nurturing environment for their children.

7. Encourage exploration - Mothers encourage their children to explore the world around them and help them develop important skills.

8. Foster creativity - Mothers help their children discover and express their creativity through activities like art, music, and storytelling.

9. Establish routines - Mothers help their children develop healthy routines and habits, such as regular bedtimes and mealtimes.

10. Nurture relationships - Mothers nurture relationships with their children and teach them the importance of developing meaningful connections with others.

Sharing custody of children, also known as joint custody, is a type of custody arrangement that allows both parents to have equal rights in making decisions about their child's upbringing and to have equal amounts of time spent with the child. This type of arrangement is typically seen when parents are not living together but both have a desire to remain actively involved in their child's life. It can also be beneficial when both parents are living together and are able to cooperate and communicate to make decisions about their child's needs.

Fathers may have custody concerns due to a variety of reasons, including wanting to ensure the safety and well-being of their child and wanting to have a meaningful role in their child's life. Fathers may also be concerned about the custodial arrangements not being fair or equitable to all parties involved.

Additionally, fathers may have concerns about the financial costs associated with being a custodial parent. Ultimately, it is important to remember that each family's situation is unique, and each parent has their own reasons and motivations for wanting to be involved in their child's life. You can request a free consultation for father's role by going to **www.kingdomjourney2healing.com.**

- Establishing paternity
- Divorce/separation
- Child support
- Visitation rights and times
- Relocation of the custodial parent
- Decision-making authority
- Parenting plans
- Grandparent visitation rights
- Modifications to existing custody orders
- Dealing with parental alienation.

Here are some questions to ask and seek clarity as to the concerns for fathers:

1. What type of custody arrangement is best for the child?
2. What are the rights and responsibilities of each parent in a custody arrangement?
3. How will the child be supported financially?
4. What kind of visitation schedule works best for the child and the parents?
5. How will decisions be made regarding the child's welfare?

6. How will communication between the parents and the child be maintained?
7. How will holidays and special occasions be shared?
8. How will the child's education be handled?
9. How will medical and religious decisions be handled?
10. How will changes to the custody arrangement be handled?

Mothers have custody concerns because they often have the primary responsibility for the care of their children. This can involve physical and mental health care, education, and other aspects of their children's lives. Additionally, many mothers have a strong emotional connection to their children, which can make it difficult for them to contemplate any kind of shared custody arrangement. It is important to remember that all parents should have the opportunity to be involved in their children's lives, and that mother's should have the same legal rights as fathers when it comes to custody concerns. You can request a free consultation for mother's role by going to www.kingdomjourney2healing.com. Here are some examples of concerns for mothers:

- Legal rights: Mothers should make sure they understand their legal rights as a custodial parent and what the court is likely to decide in their specific case.
- Visitation: Visitation is a key issue for mothers to consider when it comes to child custody. How often and when the non-custodial parent will see the child should be discussed.
- Financial Support: Mothers need to consider how the court will determine financial support and how they will enforce the non-custodial parent paying it.

- Education: Decisions must be made about the child's education, including whether they will attend a public or private school and who will pay for it.
- Health Care: Mothers need to decide who will be responsible for providing health care for the child, including insurance and medical bills.
- Relocation: Mothers should consider what would happen if they or the non-custodial parent wanted to move away.
- Religion: Mothers should think about how the court will decide on religious upbringing, if it is an issue.
- Grandparents' Rights: Mothers should consider what rights grandparents have when it comes to visitation and custody.
- Emergencies: Mothers should determine who will take care of the child in case of an emergency.
- Parental Rights: Mothers should understand their parental rights and the rights of the non-custodial parent when it comes to child custody.

Here are some questions to ask and seek clarity as to the concerns for mothers:

1. What are the child's current living arrangements?
2. Who will make decisions about the child's education and health care?
3. How can the child's relationship with both parents be maintained and promoted?
4. How will financial support of the child be provided?
5. What is the best parenting plan to meet the child's needs?
6. Will there be any restrictions on the parent's access to the child?
7. What type of visitation schedule should be established?
8. How will holidays and other special occasions be observed?
9. What is the most suitable way to resolve any disputes?
10. How can the child's best interests be protected?

A strong foundation in families can bring many positive benefits, such as providing a supportive network, teaching important values, and promoting long-term success. A strong family foundation can offer a strong sense of identity and belonging, help create and maintain positive relationships, and provide a safe environment for healthy development. It can also help instill important values, such as respect, responsibility, integrity, and hard work. When these values are embraced and instilled in family life, they can lead to greater success in the future, such as better academic performance and increased career opportunities. A strong family foundation can also provide an emotional support system, which is especially important in times of difficulty or stress. Ultimately, a strong foundation in families can help promote overall well-being and success for individuals and families.

The family has been greatly influenced by the role of grandparents and extended relatives. Throughout history, grandparents have played an important role in providing support, guidance, and love to their grandchildren. In many cases, grandparents served as surrogate parents or helped to supplement the parenting of their own children. In some cases, grandparents were the primary caregivers of their grandchildren due to parents being away from home due to work or other commitments. Grandparents were often seen as a source of stability, wisdom, and security and were respected and admired within the community. They would often pass on values, traditions and culture to their grandchildren, creating a sense of continuity between generations. They also provided a strong foundation for their grandchildren to form strong relationships and build a strong sense of identity. Overall, grandparents have a long and important history of providing love, support, and guidance to their grandchildren. They have been and continue to be an invaluable part of the family structure.

In recent years, grandparents have had limited involvement due to the systemic issues of poverty and migration further apart from relatives. This is largely linked to poor human relationships and a false sense of independence from each other. The truth is, it takes a village to raise the children.

Grandparents and extended relatives can play an important role in assisting to raise the next generation of American children. Parenting across multiple generations can be both an exciting and challenging experience. It's important to remember that the values and beliefs of each generation may be different, but each should be respected. Parenting is no different and can involve a variety of approaches, from more traditional values to more progressive ones. It's important to maintain an open dialogue between all members of a multigenerational family and to understand that each generation has something valuable to contribute. Respectful communication and understanding should be at the heart of any multigenerational family, and parenting is no different.

Grandparents and extended family members are invaluable to our lives. They provide us with a sense of stability, an understanding of our culture and heritage, and a connection to our past. They can provide us with advice, guidance, wisdom, and an extra layer of love and support. Grandparents and extended family can also be a great source of fun and entertainment and can provide us with a unique perspective on life and how to navigate it. All in all, grandparents and extended family can be a tremendous source of comfort and joy in our lives.

As we close this chapter, I want to remind you of this simple question.

**What is the role of a parent? A parent is to:**

- Protect your child from harm;
- Provide your child with food, clothing and a place to live;
- Provide financial support to your child or children;

- **Provide safety, supervision and control.**

When relationships end, break up, or terminate, neither party can "run" the other household. When safety is compromised, there are professionals who serve as neutral parties involved. Child Welfare, Courts, Mediators, Lawyers, and other community partners can be involved when safety is the issue. Technically, we "mind our own business," unless there is an issue of safety.

## WHAT IS MENTAL HEALTH, WHO ARE THE PROVIDERS, AND WHY IS IT IMPORTANT?

Many people have gone through very tragic history of generational and historical trauma. Many parented through the trauma and never truly healed. It starts with you to strengthen our community. Accessing culturally competent professional licensed therapist is part of that journey. I want to use this chapter just to explain what mental health is. You may have noticed that throughout this book I suggested that you talk to a licensed clinical social worker or therapist. This is mental health therapy. Relationship challenges are part of your mental health. What is mental health therapy? Mental health therapy is a form of treatment used to help people manage and cope with mental health issues. It typically involves talking to a therapist about your thoughts, feelings, and experiences in order to gain insight and learn coping strategies. It is paid for on a cash basis or by insurance. Through mental health therapy, you can gain the skills and confidence to better understand and manage the challenges that arise in life. By managing your emotions, you make sound decisions as a parent. Mental health therapy can be extremely helpful in helping people to better manage their mental health. It can provide a safe and supportive environment where people can discuss their feelings and experiences, and learn to identify and regulate their emotions. It can also provide tools and strategies to help people cope with difficult situations, better manage stress, and build resilience. Ultimately, therapy can help people to feel more in control of their mental health and lead a more fulfilling and meaningful life.

Mental health professionals are mental health experts who provide services to individuals and families to help them manage mental health issues. Check credentials as some coaches are not licensed therapist. In the age were everyone declares to be relationship coaches, parent coaches, or divorce coaches, licensed professionals are supervised by the State and best practices of clinical intervention. There is a code of ethics for ensuring the health and wellness of the public good.

Licensed professional help includes:
- Licensed Clinical Social Workers (LCSW)
- Marriage and Family Therapists (MFT)
- Psychologists
- Student Therapist, such as Associate Clinical Social Worker or Marriage and Family Intern

There are forms of professional help that are not therapist, but can be helpful. They are:

- Domestic Violence Counselors
- Substance Abuse Counselors
- Psychiatrists (prescribe medication)
- Pastoral Care

Each of these professionals has a unique set of qualifications, and the type of professional you choose will depend on your particular needs. It is important to speak to a few professionals in order to determine which one is the best fit for you and your situation. Mental Health Providers will each have a style and clinical modality that they prefer to use. Therapist can be helpful in many ways:

- Listen to parents with an open mind and provide a safe and non-judgmental space for them to talk about their concerns.
- Help parents identify and manage their emotions, as well as the emotions of their children.
- Educate parents on the importance of positive parenting and provide tips and strategies to help them be successful.
- Assist parents in understanding their children's behavior and provide guidance on how to respond in a helpful and effective way.
- Assist parents in developing a clear and consistent discipline system that works for their family.
- Help parents build a strong and healthy relationship with their children.
- Offer guidance on how to set appropriate boundaries and expectations for their children.

- Help parents develop effective communication and problem-solving skills.
- Offer tools and techniques to help parents manage their stress and build resilience.
- Help parents learn how to identify and address issues of anxiety, depression, and other mental health concerns.
- Assist parents in developing healthy coping skills to use when faced with difficult or challenging situations.
- Provide information to parents about community resources and how to access them.
- Assist parents in building a support network of family and friends.
- Help parents understand the impact of divorce or separation to their children.
- Work with parents to create an action plan for dealing with difficult or challenging behavior.
- Offer guidance to parents on how to handle difficult conversations with their children.
- Assist parents in understanding the importance of self-care and provide tips on how to practice it.
- Help parents to identify their strengths and weaknesses and how to build on them.
- Assist parents in understanding the impact of their own upbringing and how it affects their parenting.
- Provide resources and tools to parents to help them advocate for their children in school and other settings.

As I close this chapter, I want to share a valuable resource. I discovered a little book by Don Miguel Ruiz called the Four Agreements. The Four Agreements is based on the wisdom of the Toltecs, an indigenous people of Mexico who preceded the Aztecs. Ruiz draws on shamanic teachings and combines these with modern insights to provide a guide to freedom and well-being, based around four moral pillars. This reveals the source of self-limiting beliefs that rob us of joy and create needless suffering in these principles. The Four Agreements are:

**Be Impeccable With Your Word.**
**Don't Take Anything Personally.**
**Don't Make Assumptions.**
**Always Do Your Best.**

These principles have help me in both personal and professional spaces. Parenting is a tough job. It does not come with a manual for success. Sharing this already difficult role with a person you do not like may seem like an impassable mountain. There is hope. What is your legacy? By maintaining and managing emotions, mastering individuality, modeling being a good enough human being, and remembering the success strategies, of your mission to build a strong kid to take on the world, and make the world a better place can happen. Live your best life so you child can live theirs!

# TYPES OF TRAUMATIC EXPERIENCES

The National Traumatic Stress Network has strived to provide definitions of types of traumatic events. There are differences between them based on the event, who was involved, and even the law. In short, you may have lived through one or many of these events. Here are descriptions of the core types of trauma:

**Sexual Abuse or Assault:** Actual or attempted sexual contact, exposure to age-inappropriate sexual material or environments, sexual exploitation, unwanted or coercive sexual contact.

**Physical Abuse or Assault:** Actual or attempted infliction of physical pain with or without use of an object or weapon and including use of severe corporeal punishment.

**Emotional Abuse/Psychological Maltreatment:** Acts of commission against a minor child, other than physical or sexual abuse, that caused or could have caused conduct, cognitive, affective or other mental disturbance, such as verbal abuse, emotional abuse, excessive demands on a child's performance that may lead to negative self-image and disturbed behavior. Acts of omission against a minor child that caused or could have caused conduct, cognitive, affective or other mental disturbance, such as emotional neglect or intentional social deprivation.

**Neglect:** Failure by the child victim's caretaker(s) to provide needed, age-appropriate care although financially able to do so, or offered financial or other means to do so, including physical neglect, medical neglect, or educational neglect.

**Serious Accident or Illness/Medical Procedure:** Unintentional injury or accident, having a physical illness or experiencing medical procedures that are extremely painful and/or life threatening.

**Witness to Domestic Violence:** Exposure to emotional abuse, actual/attempted physical or sexual assault, or aggressive control perpetrated between a parent/caretaker and another adult in the child victim's home environment or perpetrated by an adolescent against one or more adults in the child victim's home environment.

**Victim/Witness to Community Violence:** Extreme violence in the community, including exposure to gang-related violence.

**School Violence:** Violence that occurs in a school setting, including, but not limited to school shootings, bullying, interpersonal violence among classmates, and classmate suicide.

**Natural or Manmade Disasters**: Major accident or disaster that is an unintentional result of a manmade or natural event.

**Forced Displacement:** Forced relocation to a new home due to political reasons, generally including political asylees or immigrants fleeing political persecution.

**War/Terrorism/Political Violence**: Exposure to acts of war/terrorism/political violence including incidents such bombing, shooting, looting, or accidents that are a result of terrorist activity as well as actions of individuals acting in isolation if they are considered political in nature.

**Victim/Witness to Extreme Personal/Interpersonal Violence:** Includes extreme violence by or between individuals including exposure to homicide, suicide and other similar extreme events.

**Traumatic Grief/Separation:** Death of a parent, primary caretaker or sibling, abrupt and/or unexpected, accidental or premature death or homicide of a close friend, family member, or other close relative; abrupt, unexplained and/or indefinite separation from a parent, primary caretaker or sibling due to circumstances beyond the child victim's.

**System-Induced Trauma:** Traumatic removal from the home, traumatic foster placement, sibling separation, or multiple placements in a short amount of time.

*(Adapted from National Child Traumatic Stress Network, 2008)*

If you have experienced any of these traumatic events, please consider a conversation with a licensed therapist. Licensed therapists include:

- Licensed Clinical Social Worker (LCSW)
- Licensed Professional Counselor (LPC)
- Marriage and Family Therapist (MFT)
- Student Therapists: Associate Clinical Social Worker (ACSW) & Marriage and Family Therapist Intern (MFTI)
- Psychologist
- Psychiatrists

Other Professionals you may find are:

- Pastoral Counselors
- Certified Peer Specialist
- Alcohol & Drug Abuse Counselor
- Domestic Violence Counselors

# It's okay to ask for help.

# COMMUNITY RESOURCES

Child Welfare Information Gateway (www.childwelfare.gov) provides resources for understanding Child Abuse and Neglect. Here are resources that Child Welfare Information Gateway provides if you suspect that a child's health or safety is jeopardized due to abuse or neglect by parents or other caretaker who has custody of the child, contact the child protective services agency in your county. Trained social workers staff these 24-hour Hotlines. If you are reporting suspected child abuse or neglect regarding children in another county please contact that county's child protective services agency.

Child Abuse/Childhelp®
Phone: 800.4.A.CHILD (800.422.4453)
People They Help: Child abuse victims, parents, concerned individuals

Child Sexual Abuse-Darkness to Light
Phone: 866.FOR.LIGHT (866.367.5444)
People They Help: Children and adults needing local information or resources about sexual abuse

Family Violence-National Domestic Violence Hotline
Phone: 800.799.SAFE (800.799.7233)
TTY: 800.787.3224
Video Phone Only for Deaf Callers: 206.518.9361
People They Help: Children, parents, friends, offenders

Help for Parent-National Parent Helpline®
Phone: 855.4APARENT (855.427.2736) (available 10 a.m. to 7 p.m., PST, weekdays)
People They Help: Parents and caregivers needing emotional support and links to resources

Human Trafficking-National Human Trafficking Hotline
Phone: 888.373.7888
People They Help: Victims of human trafficking and those reporting potential trafficking situations

Mental Illness-National Alliance on Mental Illness
Phone: 800.950.NAMI (800.950.6264) (available 10 a.m. to 6 p.m., ET, weekdays)
People They Help: Individuals, families, professionals

Missing/Abducted Children-Child Find of America
Phone: 800.I.AM.LOST (800.426.5678)
People They Help: Parents reporting lost or abducted children, including parental abductions

Child Find of America—Mediation
Phone: 800.A.WAY.OUT (800.292.9688)
People They Help: Parents (abduction, prevention, child custody issues)

National Center for Missing and Exploited Children
Phone: 800.THE.LOST (800.843.5678)
TTY: 800.826.7653
People They Help: Families and professionals (social services, law enforcement)

Rape/Incest-Rape, Abuse and Incest National Network (RAINN)
Phone: 800.656.HOPE (800.656.4673)
People They Help: Rape and incest victims, media, policymakers, concerned individuals

Substance Abuse-National Alcoholism and Substance Abuse Information Center
Phone: 800.784.6776
People They Help: Families, professionals, media, policymakers, concerned individuals

Suicide Prevention-National Suicide Prevention Lifeline
Phone: 800.273.TALK (800.273.8255)
TTY: 800.799.4TTY (800.799.4889)
People They Help: Families, concerned individuals


Youth in Trouble/Runaways-National Runaway Switchboard
Phone: 800.RUNAWAY (800.786.2929)
People They Help: Runaway and homeless youth, families

# EMERGENCY RESPONSE NUMBERS

*California County Emergency Response Child Abuse Reporting Telephone Numbers*

| | |
|---|---|
| Alameda County | (510)-259-1800 |
| Alpine County | (530)-694-2235 |
| Amador County | (209)-223-6550 – Mon thru Thurs 8:00-5:00 (209)-223-1075 – After hours |
| Butte County | (530)-538-7882 (800)-400-0902 – 24 hours |
| Calaveras County | (209)-754-6452 (209)-754-6500 – After hours |
| Colusa County | (530)-458-0280 |
| Contra Costa County | (877)-881-1116 |
| Del Norte County | (707)-464-3191 |
| El Dorado County | (530)-642-7100 – Placerville (530)-573-3201 – South Lake Tahoe |
| Fresno County | (559)-255-8320 |
| Glenn County | (530)-934-6520 (530)-934-6519 (530)-934-1429 – Intake |
| Humboldt County | (707)-445-6180 |
| Imperial County | (760)-337-7750 |
| Inyo County | (760)-872-1727 |
| Kern County | (661)-631-6011 (760)-375-6049 |

| | |
|---|---|
| Kings County | (559)-582-3241 – 8:00-5:00<br>(559)-582-8776 – After hours<br>(866)-582-8776 |
| Lake County | (707)-262-0235<br>(800)-386-4090 |
| Lassen County | (530)-251-8277<br>(530)-257-6121<br>(530) 260-8131 – After hours |
| Los Angeles County | (800)-540-4000 – Within CA<br>(213)-639-4500 – Outside CA<br>(800)-272-6699 – TDD<br>Online Reporting:<br>https://reportChildAbuseLA.org |
| Madera County | (559)-675-7829<br>(800)-801-3999 |
| Marin County | (415)-473-7153 |
| Mariposa County | (209)-742-0900 – Daytime<br>(209)-966-7000 – After hours |
| Mendocino County | (707)-463-7992 – Ukiah<br>(707)-962-1100 – Fort Bragg<br>(866)-263-0368 – Toll free |
| Merced County | (209)-385-3104 |
| Modoc County | (530)-233-6602<br>(866)-233-4424 |
| Mono County | (760)-924-1770<br>(760)-932-7549 – Sheriff Office<br>(800)-340-5411 – Hot Line |
| Monterey County | (831)-755-4661<br>(800)-606-6618 |
| Napa County | (707)-253-4262<br>(707)-253-4261<br>(800)-464-4216 |

| | |
|---|---|
| Nevada County | (530)-273-4291 – 24 hour |
| Orange County | (714)-940-1000<br>(800)-207-4464 |
| Placer County | (916)-872-6549<br>(866)-293-1940 |
| Plumas County | (530)-283-6300 – Sheriff Office<br>(530)-283-6350<br>(800)-242-3338 – Toll free |
| Riverside County | (800)-442-4918<br>(877)-922-4453 |
| Sacramento County | (916)-875-5437 |
| San Benito County | (831)-636-4190<br>(831)-636-4330 – After hours Police |
| San Bernardino County | (909)-384-9233<br>(800)-827-8724 |
| San Diego County | (858)-560-2191<br>(800)-344-6000 |
| San Francisco County | (415)-558-2650<br>(800)-856-5553 |
| San Joaquin County | (209)-468-1333 |
| San Luis Obispo County | (805)-781-5437<br>(800)-834-5437 |
| San Mateo County | (650)-595-7922<br>(650)-802-7922<br>(800)-632-4615 |
| Santa Barbara County | (800)-367-0166 |

| | |
|---|---|
| Santa Clara County | (650)-493-1186 – North<br>(408)-683-0601 – South<br>(408)-299-2071 – Central |
| Shasta County | (530)-225-5144 |
| Sierra County | (530)-289-3720<br>(530)-993-6720 |
| Siskiyou County | (530)-841-4200<br>(530)-842-7009 – 24 hour<br>hot line |
| Solano County | (800)-544-8696 |
| Sonoma County | (707)-565-4304<br>(800) 870-7064 |
| Stanislaus County | (209)-558-3665<br>(800)-558-3665 |
| Sutter County | (530)-822-7227 |
| Tehama County | (530)-527-1911<br>(800)-323-7711 |
| Trinity County | (530)-623-1314 |
| Tulare County | (800)-331-1585 |
| Tuolumne County | (209)-533-5717<br>(209)-533-4357 – After hours |
| Ventura County | (805)-654-3200 |
| Yolo County | (530)-669-2345<br>(530)-669-2346<br>(888)-400-0022 – After hours |
| Yuba County | (530)-749-6288 |

## ADDITIONAL RESOURCES

# If you or someone you care about is in crisis, take action with one of the following resources:

- Reach out to a trusted friend (or adult if you are a teenager)
- Call the National Suicide Prevention Lifeline at 1-800-273-8255
- Connect with the free Crisis Text Line: Text "NAMI" to 741741; you will text with a counselor
- Call the Trans Lifeline at 1-877-565-8860
- Call the GLBT National Hotline at 1-888-843-4564
- Call the GLBT National Youth Talkline at 1-800-246-7743
- Call the National Sexual Assault Hotline at 1-800-656-4673
- Call the National Domestic Violence Hotline at 1-800-799-7233
- Call the Veterans Crisis Line at 1-800-273-2855
- Kids' Helpline716-834-11441-877-KIDS-400
- National Postpartum Depression Warmline: 1-800-PPD-MOMS

**In an emergency, go to the nearest emergency room at your local hospital or dial "911"**

# SAMPLE FAMILY RULES

1.  God placed Parents in charge. If you have an argument, see God (PRAYER).

2.  Teenagers who need money will work for it. Car Wash, $5 (outside) $5 (inside), Special Yard project, $5, or other special assignments as requested. (1 Timothy v. 18 :The Laborer is worthy of his reward)

3.  Teenagers must clean up after themselves. Cups, plates, forks, etc should find themselves washed after use.

4.  All activities outside the home must be approved by parents. (BEFORE PLANNING OR DOING THEM)

5.  All teenagers, Monday through Friday must show proof that homework is being done to have the opportunity to work for money or privileges on the weekend. Grades must be maintained at a minimum 2.0 with no fails. Final report card grades earn: A=$20, B=$5.00

6.  All teenagers must be home by 7:30pm, Monday through Thursday, complete homework, iron clothes, bath, and prepare for the next day.

7.  TV and video games will be left available when the Parents see that the Basic Family Chores (Kitchen, Living Room, and Bathroom) are left clean at the end of each day. Laundry is done as needed and when the Parent declares the trip to laundry mat or the Teen requests to wash clothes on site.

8.  All teenagers must provide to parents a list of friends and their contact numbers (so parents can establish contact with friend's parents/monitor where you go)

9.  Teenagers must use a respectful tone when engaging with parents. Arguing loudly is not allowed, but a rational thought process can be discussed. (Honor your mother and father)

10. There will be a ZERO tolerance for breaking any of the basic rules. Privileges and money will be suspended.

# About the Author

With over 29 years of professional experience as a licensed clinical social worker, community activist, trainer, therapist, mentor, ally, and advocate, LaLisa Morgan supports her clients to be the best version of yourself as you heal from trauma and life limiting beliefs and deeply rooted family and social barriers as you develop your career and professional identity. LaLisa is an alumnus of California State University, Los Angeles where she completed her Master's Degree in Social Work, Master's Degree Health Care Management, and Certificate in Applied Gerontology. She completed her undergraduate program in Public Administration at California State University, Dominguez Hills. Additionally, LaLisa currently serves her community as a Supervising Children's Social Worker in Child Welfare for fifteen years, ensuring child safety, building families, and strengthening communities. LaLisa leads a rewarding twenty-eight-year professional career in the fields of child welfare, aging and disabled adults, and empowering youth in Los Angeles County. In her spare time, she has volunteered for many causes such as Commissioner of Human Relations for the City of Azusa, SEIU Local 721 Steward, and Academic Field Instructor for Social Work and clinical supervision for upcoming therapists..

LaLisa has been included in several anthologies that include Entrepreneurial Women of Faith: Sharing the Scriptures We Use to Keep Us Anchored to, Focused On, and Motivated in Our Businesses (Book 1), Mothers, Daughters, and Faith (Book 2), Faith Is (Book 3), The Healed Woman and Silent No More. She also has her own published work, "Surviving the Chaos: Journey to Healing and Legacy Living and companion Guided Reflection Journal. She writes to encourage other to live a life for Christ and become generational curse breakers.

LaLisa provides psychotherapy and counseling for adults in transition, men/women individual therapy, and couples therapy to help develop positive coping strategies for anxiety, depression, trauma, unhealthy relationship dynamics, and working through life's peaks and valleys during life's transitions: young adult (18-30), prenatal and postpartum, parenting, and aging. In therapy, clients are genuinely "seen and heard" while cultivating change through insight and application of new skills. LaLisa has found that her divine purpose is to guide individuals to their life purpose and self-awareness to achieve a vision of life, love, family, and community one person at a time.

www.kingdomjourney2healing.com
Instagram: KingdomJourney2Healing1865
Facebook: @Journey2healinglosangeles
Contact Information:
Telephone: (626) 862-3837
Email: journey2healingla@gmail.com

# CREATE A CALM AND RELAXING HOME ATMOSTPHERE WITH NATURAL PRODUCTS

## About doTERRA

What Does doTERRA Mean? Founded in 2008, doTERRA's mission from the beginning was to share the highest quality essential oils with the world. Having seen the incredible benefits of using these precious resources, a group of healthcare and business professionals set out to make that mission a reality. They formed a company and named it DOTERRA, a Latin derivative meaning "Gift of the Earth." The first hurdle they needed to overcome was to establish a quality standard in an industry that had never had one previously. The doTERRA founders were committed to providing only the purest, highest-grade essential oils. This commitment led to the creation of a new standard of quality: CPTG Certified Pure Tested Grade™. Every doTERRA oil is held to the highest possible level of purity.

Now, doTERRA means more than "Gift of the Earth." It means wellness, healing, and hope.

## I AM YOUR WELLNESS ADVOCATE.

Do'Terra Wellness Advocate: Essential Oils, natural products infused with essential oil products offer natural solutions for you and your loved ones.

LaLisa Morgan, LCSW

Explore products and become a member today!

my.doterra.com/gen1865journey2healing

(626) 862-3837

# OTHER BOOKS BY THE AUTHOR

**Surviving the Chaos: A Journey to Healing and Legacy Living**

Surviving the Chaos: A Journal for Healing and Legacy Living is a book designed to be read by all persons on a quest for knowledge and wisdom, to heal from the mental pain or distress in their lives. By applying the Legacy Lessons that are shared by the author, the reader will empower themselves on a healing journey and build a foundation of their identity and purpose for their future. By reading this book, the reader will:

- Establish a new foundation based on your beliefs and values.
- Learn who you are and examine your past and what you need to heal from.
- Renew your mind by applying the seven legacy life lessons.
- Find your purpose by completing reflection activities and journaling.

**Available on Amazon in paperback and eBook formats**

## Surviving the Chaos: Guided Reflection Journal

Surviving the Chaos: Guided Reflection Journal is the companion to the book, Surviving the Chaos: A Journey to Healing and Legacy Living. The journal is designed to help the reader reflect of the core principles discussed in the Life Legacy Lessons. By applying the Legacy Lessons that are shared by the author, the reader will empower themselves on a healing journey and build a foundation of their identity and purpose for their future. By reading this book, the reader will:

•Establish a new foundation based on your beliefs and values.
•Learn who you are and examine your past and what you need to heal from.
•Renew your mind by applying the seven legacy life lessons.
•Find your purpose by completing reflection activities and journaling.

### Available on Amazon in paperback.

## Silent No More: My Story, My Truth

The darkness in her eye represents her past. The light in her eye represents her future. The tear on her face represents the pain she endured. The story represents her freedom and healing. Silent No More is an anthology about childhood trauma. The authors are women who experienced horrific abuse and mistreatment when they should have been protected & cherished. They were violated, as minors. They were threatened to keep it secret and forced to keep quiet. Featuring Anjanette Robinson, Brandi Marsh, Carra Dixon, Danniel S. Withers, Jaynel Jones, LaLisa Morgan, Lucretia Y. Hayes, Melanie Rossum, Melissa McGill, Porsche Williams, Tanya DeFreitas, Vernita Edwards, and Lead Author Venus Chandler, with a bonus entry by Terry Chandler. As adults, these women are reclaiming their liberty and victory by telling their story, their truth. It's not an easy read, but it was not an easy journey to get to the place of being able to share what they experienced. Together, they are breaking the silence and they are Silent No More!

## The Healed Woman

*The Healed Woman* is the vision of two-time Amazon bestselling author, Browniesha Blackman, and it is a testament of 12 women who never imagined being broken, abandoned, and left to die in their mess. They each faced many challenges, yet they fought their way through. Now, they can say, "I was once broken but now I am whole. I once was in a trial but now I've triumphed. I once was in darkness but now God has brought me into His marvelous light.

*The Healed Woman* features a foreword by international, bestselling author, Tanya DeFreitas, and testimonies by the following women of faith: Browniesha Blackman, Ebony A. Smith, Edneisha Lee, Kadana Bryant, LaLisa Morgan, Laneice Joseph, Myisha S. Luebrun, Princess Mapp, Robyn Williams, Shae Clark, Tamika Jones, and Tinya Lewis.

A program of Generations 1865: Counseling, Consulting, & Coaching:

# KINGDOM JOURNEY TO HEALING

### Therapy can help resolve and find solutions to life's drama and trauma!

- **SINGLENESS/DATING**
- **PARENTING/CUSTODY CHALLENGES**
- **PARENTING ADULT WITH SPECIAL NEEDS**
- **RELATIONSHIP ISSUES**
- **SHARED PARENTING & CUSTODY**
- **MANHOOD/FATHERHOOD**
- **CARING FOR AGING PARENTS**
- **LIFE TRANSITIONS**
- **SEARCHING FOR IDENTITY**

Are you looking to find solutions for life issues? A neutral person is often a non-judgmental solution to talking to friends and family. Therapeutic support can help support through depression, anxiety, trauma, or other mental health challenges. Relationship challenges effects mental health!

**LET'S TALK!! Our program and services help you to make progress in life.**

- Counseling & Psychotherapy for individuals, couples, & families to improve social & romantic relationships as well as individual growth, healing, and trauma informed care;
- Specializing in supporting Relationship Roles including Singleness, Couples
- Marriage/Cohabitation, Perinatal/Preparing for Children, Men's Wellness, Aging/Life Transitions, and Parenting/Shared Parenting Responsibilities

### APPOINTMENTS AVAILABLE ONLINE (VIRTUAL)
**Email, Call or Text for your appointment.**

Program Administrator: LaLisa Morgan, MS, MSW, LCSW

Website: kingdomjourney2healing.com

## Matthew 5:14-16 MSG

"Here's another way to put it: You're here to be light, bringing out the God-colors in the world. God is not a secret to be kept. We're going public with this, as public as a city on a hill. If I make you light-bearers, you don't think I'm going to hide you under a bucket, do you? I'm putting you on a light stand. Now that I've put you there on a hilltop, on a light stand----shine!! Keep opening up to others, you'll prompt people to open up with God, this generous Father in Heaven."